I0107823

# Schizophrenic Lullabies

# Schizophrenic Lullabies

## By
## Fritz O'Skennick

Cover Artwork & Photography
By
Jayde Antonin

Copyright of Richard Banbury
ISBN: 978-1-4475-2359-8

## Dedicated to Shaun & Romana

Thank you to my Mum & Dad for all their support and thank you also to Will & Adam for their support, suggestions & encouragement…

And a HUGE thank you to Jayde, for creating the cover pictures & for his continuing tolerance, support & encouragement with all my wacky projects…

And indeed thank you to you, the reader without whom this book would not be possible…

# Contents

# Foreword

**"Schizophrenic Lullabies"** is an insightful and revealing collection of dark poetry themed in the realms of mental illness as expressed with such startling clarity and profound depth in the unique style of dark writer, poet and mental health sufferer, **Fritz O'Skennick.**

Now for the first time in one volume, **"Schizophrenic Lullabies"** past, present and previously unpublished collide in an engaging and captivating anthology.

This collection features dark poetry and prose that delve deep into the mindsets and madness of schizophrenia, Bipolar, depression, voices, delusions and self harm, while also skimming over addiction and suicidal thoughts.

Now in celebration of Fritz's 40th birthday comes this often requested and definitive collection *(definitive to the time of publication)* of poems that many have come to love and be inspired by via books, performance and postings on popular poetry site, Allpoetry.com.

    **Fritz O'Skennick** is an accomplished creative artist and writer with many strings to his bow. As a singer/songwriter, poet, novelist, playwright/actor & performer, he has enjoyed varying successes with a number of his projects.

    Previously published, some of his lighter work has appeared in various anthologies with other poets as produced by United Press.

His solo debut into literary publication was **"Touching the Darkness"** a highly anticipated anthology of his dark poetry that concentrates solely on his darker work that many have come to enjoy via Allpoetry.com and via performances throughout Wales and parts of England.

His second book **"Fear the Reaper"** is a unique, intense, first-person psychological crime thriller that tells a schizophrenic tale of love, loss, revenge and madness.

This was quickly followed by his third book **"The Darkness Verses The Light"** which is a mixed genre collection of poetry, prose and short stories.

His fourth book **"Who is John Doe?"** is a unique supernatural drama based on his popular stage show of the same name.

His fifth book **"Of Darkness and Light"** is a collection of poetry and prose, featuring new work and also many outstanding collaborative works with fellow poets from all over the World, including a collaboration that features no less than 40 poets in 1 poem as orchestrated and edited by Fritz.

His sixth book **"Dark Confessions"** is an intense serial killer novella and concentrates on the darker nature of man, exploring the facets and mind states of murder, revenge and the lengths we'd go to in the name of love, honor and redemption...

His seventh book **"Gothic Tales"** is a definitive collection of his ever popular supernatural poetry, featuring vampires, werewolves, ghost stories, murder, immortality and various other themes based in science fiction and fantasy.

His debut album **"UNspokeN"** (music) was released on Petrified Records in 2005 amidst a string of impressive reviews and radio play all over the world.

Playwright and acting credits include **"It could Happen to You"** and **"Who is John Doe?"** as produced by the former theatre company "Progress Cymru".

He is presently working on a second album of his music **"UNbrokeN",** his new book **"Just the Lyrics"** and writing his new series of sci-fi books **"Temporal Medium"**.

For further details of his poetry go to
http://allpoetry.com/Fritz%20O%20skennick

For further details of his music go to
http://www.myspace.com/fracturedpersona

For further details of his performance poetry go to
http://www.myspace.com/fritzo39skennick

# Schizophrenic Lullabies & Bipolar Berceuse… (Rhyme)

# Darkness Rising.

Darkness rising, calls to me,
Be still, my beating heart.
Hate subsiding, leave me be,
The darkness is my art.
Embracing darkest thoughts within,
A door that stands ajar.
Chasing childhood fantasies,
So near and yet so far.

To touch upon the darkest mind,
My fingers numb with cold.
I touch upon a world within,
And feel its grip take hold.
Chattered teeth and numbing pain,
My flesh is torn apart.
I feel reborn inside my mind,
Embrace my lonely heart.

The door I spoke of stays ajar,
So soon to open wide.
Engulf me in its blanket cold,
With no where warm to hide.
Each time I leave, is harder still,
To tear away and roam.
The saddest truth of all to bare,
Within my mind, I'm home.

# Twixt the Darkness and the Light...

Walking on a shadowed path,
twixt Darkness and the Light.
A solitude that screams aloud
and haunts my wakeful nights.

Demons feed upon my soul,
corrupt my thoughts to lies.
Voices calling out my name
are drowned amidst my cries.

Blood that drips from fingers clenched,
unsure if its my own.
Darkness seeing through my eyes
that taints me to the bone.

Blade for carving rictus grins
in flesh so soft and warm.
Be my prey, this night, my love,
embrace my passion's storm.

Let me be your fantasy,
and feel me bleed you dry.
Making love, life ebbs away,
I feel your spirit fly.

Weakened to your pallid corpse,
for life and lust is spent.
Tears are welling in my eyes,
behold my dark descent.

I shake my head, it fades away,
another damn illusion.
So lost in fictions I become,
my mind in such confusion.

So I do what I must do,
put pen to pad and write.
Create in Darkness, let it seep,
so I may walk in light.

## **<u>Darkling Darlings (Acrostic)...</u>**

Delving deep beyond my thoughts,
As demons shriek their rage.
Reeling as my dreams are caught,
Kept twix't my mind and page.
Living in delusions grasp,
I feel the darkness rise.
Nevermore I plead agasp,
Grind down this wall of lies.

Does illusion have a face?
At one with all my doubts.
Raging angel's fall from grace,
Lay down thy seasoned shouts.
In a world of empty souls,
No loss, this life I own.
Gestalt, my mind and thunder roll,
So cold, my heart of stone.

# Dark Delusions...

When the darkness comes to me,
Embraced with seething rage.
Intense, neurotic daydreams creep
Within this mortal cage.
Feed delusion's waiting grasp,
And quell this passing dread.
Show me futures yet untold,
As truth within my head.

Show me souls beyond my time,
Colliding in the void.
Whisper words for me to write,
That leave me overjoyed.
Delude me with a thousand tales,
Embrace my fractured mind.
Seduce me with your fatal charms,
And see what we can find.

Overwhelmed and un-fulfilled,
I rise and face the day.
Scribe the thoughts within my mind,
As voices fade away.
Wear my mask to greet the world,
And wait, my mind at war.
For when the darkness deep inside,
Shall rise again once more.

## Dark Alphabetie Skettie: Acrostic Alphabet

And so I see as time has passed
Beyond the veil of hope
Clawing from the depths within
Defined by how I cope
Effervescent thoughts disperse
For life beholds the dreams
Growing from so deep within
How swift it always seems
Isolated from a world
Just loosely holding on
Knowing that the time will come
Let go the world that's gone
May I find the peace I seek
No more the raging voices
On the bough of fractured thoughts
Prevailing all my choices
Quake beneath the lonely nights
Raging mind be still
So my soul cries out its pain
To break the Demon's will
Understand and know my heart
Valor fades too far
Waking hours, full of fear with
Xylographic scars
Yeild before a broken mind
Zymotic thoughts bizarre

# Transcendental Mindscapes...
## (Intense Rhyme)

I find in all that I've beheld,
as time has come to pass.
My blind recall sat live yet quelled,
as I'm so numb alas.
No more the rays of rising dawn
to kiss upon my skin.
So war dismays, despising spawned
abyss forgone within.

So I wait for things to change,
untouched by all I see.
Though by hate your strings derange
and such lies fall by free.
Falling through the darkest thoughts,
unbound to any choices.
Calling to embark to naught,
confound the many voices.

Finding strength to claw away
from wraiths so deep within.
Bind the length to draw the sway
with faith that sleeps akin.
No more lonely, broken nights,
so plagued by anguished soul.
So sore, only woken blight,
though vague to languish whole.

Avail me of my wakeful dreams
that make me live illusion.
Regale me with forsake-full screams
that quake and give confusion.
So strong the pull of what's within,
it fills me with its fear.
No longer full of rotting sin,
it's will free when it's near.

Too weak to fight its growing sway,
this gift that I'm bestowed.
Unique, its might, its knowing way,
adrift in time's abode.
I see potential futures bled
beyond what fate has sown.
I free sequential suture's thread,
au fond, it waits unknown.

Lost unto my thoughts and dreams,
succumb to all I know.
Tossed into wry, wrought planned schemes,
to some, the call of woe.

# <u>The Paths within my Mind...</u>

You've asked me to unlock the door
to let you peek inside,
to show you things that lie beneath,
the secrets that I hide.
And as you've asked so nicely,
I'll guide you through my mind,
but be aware I've warned you of
the dark things you may find.

The voices call beyond the void,
the darkness seeping in,
I struggle with the Demon's will
that leads my soul to sin.
I see things in the twilight time
that draws the madness near,
the ghosts that walk peripheral,
beheld but never clear.

The visions in the dream time
become my latent curse,
that speak confusion to my eyes
to scribe fatidic verse.
The whispers in the silence
that laugh and call my name,
the shifting of reality
that sets my mind aflame.

Loneliness becomes my fate,
for none can understand
a schizophrenic's heart and soul
that rests within fate's hand.
The paths that fork and fracture thoughts
that make illusions blind.
Darkness shrouds the mindscape's sight
within my broken mind.

Numbness creeping through my hopes,
consuming all my dreams,
forever walking through this life
that's never what it seems.
Creating worlds inside my mind
while loosely holding on,
my biggest fear is when I die,
this world will soon be gone.

# Insomniatic Lullabies...

I've always had this problem,
I can't switch off my mind,
it stops me sleeping through the nights,
with all my thoughts combined.
Insomnia becomes my curse,
that drains me of my sleep,
whispers in the silence
that stop me counting sheep.

Visions in the darkness
building in my head,
voices calling me to scribe
their words so softly said,
begging me to tell their tales
and all they need to say
to make me see beyond the veil
in dreams beyond today.

Sleep becomes an issue,
in tricks before my eyes,
seeing worlds beyond my own,
revealing this one's lies.
Seeing passed the surface mask
that hides the deeper truth,
creation starts within the thoughts
that many lose in youth.

I wish that I could switch it off,
be normal for a while
to feel the things that humans feel
and things that make them smile.
Instead my life is so surreal,
I'm lost inside my head,
living in so many worlds
in fictions softly bled.

When I think of writer's block,
to me its just a dream,
something to aspire too
so life's not so extreme.
Go to sleep with clear thoughts,
with dreams where they should be
inside my head but when I wake,
I find that I'm still me…

# All That I Become...

So much that I would wish to do,
but days just pass to weeks,
and time is such a cruel mistress,
for king of all the freaks.

Weeks that pass to months and years,
my soul it grows so cold,
empty, hollow, growing numb
as voices grow so bold

Visions in the quiet time
that bid me scribe their tales,
seeing through illusion's eyes
as madness soon prevails.

I walk unseen by all around,
I live like I am dead,
a ghost who walks a lonely path
and lives inside my head.

So much that I would wish from life,
a reason to survive,
if I could hear my heart but once,
to know I'm still alive.

But I know it's not my fate,
I walk in endless night,
balancing a path between
the darkness and the light.

Always seeking who I was
to guide who I become,
holding back a demon's wrath,
ensure I don't succumb.

Please remember who I am
and all I have achieved,
wrapped in my cocoon of lies
of dreams that I believed.

My words shall live beyond my time,
please cherish all they say,
for they define the man I am
in life and death's ballet.

# Lost in Fictions...

Whispers in the quiet time
where shadows dance and play.
Lost to dreams and thoughts sublime
throughout the night and day.
The fatal flaw that is my bane,
no limit can I see.
I need to write to keep me sane,
and set these feelings free.

Creating fictions in my mind,
within, so dark and deep.
Curious to all I find,
that stops me finding sleep.
That I should find finality,
to ease the pain of being.
To breath my own reality,
a flicker of foreseeing.

Beneath the rays of rising dawn,
bequeathed that dreams may borrow.
A daylight lullaby is born,
that soothes in our tomorrow.
Shifting skies of lavender,
that bathe my tired mind.
Enthralled, behold its splendor
the dark and light entwined.

For now I write by candle light,
Immortal dreams are penned.
Before I find eternal night
and darkness without end.

# Schizophrenic Lullabies
# & Bipolar Berceuse...
# (Freeverse)

# Damaged goods...

Little pinpricks of cold
seeping through the cracks in my mind.
I hammer desperately at the cramps within,
as numbness sighs like Winter's waking breath.
It stretches it's wings in a blanket of ice,
consuming me, freezing me with it's touch.
And so I weep unseen…

Voices rage in a maelstrom of thoughts,
awakening the darkness once more.
Must it always be this way?
Always seeing, yet an empty shell in it's shadow cast.
Paralysis creeps through my cranium
like a dormant assassin, unseen, unfelt,
yet always so devastating.

I'm so alone, bestowed as I am
with these accursed demons.
I'm losing my mind,
Piece by piece, fragment by fragment,
It drains away into a void of self loathing and despair.
If I should mourn my loss of self,
Then I weep for who I was… or who I should be…

…Or who I could be…

Help me……………

# Remember me, My Love...

I pale in thy wondrous beauty,
my beloved Angel.
I hath not forsaken thee, nor would I.
Thy words, bring great solace
and comfort to my tortured soul.
But alas, these precious moments dissipate
into the ether, cherished and fading…

Mine heart breaks for thee,
My soul aches for thee,
My dreams spake of thee.
Today the king falls and humbles,
fearful in the darkness.
So desperate, so alone, so broken…
And so the madness beckons seductively.

Illusion blinds mine eyes,
Rage darkens my soul,
Eternity taunts my very essence.
Torn asunder, I bleed'eth my sanity,
into a void of orphean dreams.
Grasping for light amidst darkest thoughts,
ascending time and perception.

What was, is and could be
dilutes into despair amidst a sea of sorrows.
Nevermore may I dare to dream
of thy touch upon my skin.
Thine soulful eyes, nor thy lips
enflamed in our first passioned kiss.
But alas, I shalt always hold thee in great adoration…

Forgive me, my love…
Fore this is not of my choosing.
Darker forces conspire to usurp my mortal mind,
condemning my soul to living death.
Remember me as I am
and not the stranger I may become…
A soulless, empty shadow of former glory…

And if this truly be normality,
then I findeth I hath no taste for it…

# <u>My Madness doth spake...</u>

Ye shalt plague me no more,
yon demons of inner born.
Begone, I doth weary of thy voices'
pestilence upon my soul.
Thou hast blinded mine eyes,
with thy darkest thoughts.
Thou hast seduced me
with thine illusions of deceit.
Thou hast smothered my very essence,
in a blanket of thy madness.
But nay, thou shalt plague me no more.

Verily, I doth summon my darkness.
I shalt make'th it my own
and nevermore be a slave to thy charms.
Fore I doth decree,
that I am Lord of my demons,
Master of my soul, Keeper of my mind…
But alas, I doth crumble,
Fore sooth, I see this new found strength
for what it is… Another illusion…
And so my walls cascade in twilight shadow.

Damn it, I am undone...

# Self Loathing...

Seeing through the rage,
a veil of red
doth shroud mine eyes,
as frail minds shatter
in the cold dawn
of cascading illusion.
A penance of my madness
that does't taunt
my perceptions
in a blanket of
ill conceived ideals
and humility
in mine own flaws.

Dost thou spake of love?
Art thou enamoured
by this foul
manifestation
of fear and despair?
Personifying
all that I loathe
in dark voices
that softly whisper
their lies
in gently
layered truth.

But what if the sunset rose
and I no longer breathed
to embrace
its gentle warmth?
Would'st thou
weep for me?
Would'st thou mark
my passing?
Would'st thou
fight thy tears
behind a veil
of crimson petals?

Dousing thoughts of what could be…

## <u>One Lifetime...</u>

I create in the Darkness,
that I may walk in the light,
visions that fill my mind,
gentle whispers
in the quiet time,
that bid me scribe
such sublime
quintessence,
etching rhapsodies
bequeathed in madness,
a creator beheld
in perpetuity,
penning dreams
of our tomorrows...

*...One lifetime is never enough...*

# Release...

Circling the drain,
caught in a tidal wave
of dark truth as illusion
gently simmers below,
pulling me down,
engulfing me
in its comfort and safety.

I can't let it go...
Not yet... Please...
I beg of you...
I so desperately need
its softly spoken lies
to sedate the darkness within
and better the man
I become...

My Deity of sublime
Perfection...
My dream, my love...
Whose journey
so impossibly
mirrors my own...

Whose very essence
fills my head,
calming my demons,
warming my heart,
with tears and laughter,
I'd forgotten how to feel...

She ignites my mind,
sparking my muse
in a blaze of exquisite writes…
She inspires my soul,
beyond word or thought…

And truly,
I know I'm grasping
an impossible dream,
but its my dream
and dream I shall…

Please don't take it
away from me,
I need it so very much…

Circling the drain,
caught in a current
of dark illusion
and false clarity,
desperately
hoping
submergence
brings…

…Release…

# Fragmented Reality...

I bury my emotions,
But they keep
clawing their way
back to the surface
unbidden…

Time was,
I had control over them,
So why am I now
a serf to their
impulses?

Its happening
more and more,
breaking my heart
needlessly…
What's wrong with me?

The fallen Angel
embraced the Demon,
betrayed by a kiss
that conspires
my self destruction…

Avoidance of destiny,
tempting fate,
one time too many…
Warping reality
in a distorted
parody of life…

What is happening to me?
A bitter, jagged pill,
I swallow hard,
hoping it cuts
and poisons every tie…

Memories fade,
replaced by delusions
I crave
more than life itself...

Someone crept into my mind
as I slept,
changing all the locks
in my world...

Walls closing in...
Wounds won't heal...
The dead keep talking...
Reality keeps changing...
Make it stop, please...

This is not who I am...
This is not the world
I fell asleep in...
Subtle strands tweak
the edges of perception,
defined by all that is lost...

The tapestry unravels,
changing the picture...
And I become the demon
in my head,
reflecting a stranger's eyes
in my own blade...

Who am I?

# Mournful Lullaby...

Yesterday becomes
a fading memory,
bestowing feelings
of entropy
upon my heart...

Harsh words,
spoken in haste,
too late
to take back...

Painting such
sorrowful blight
on the canvas
of my soul
as love decays
in a string
of broken promises...

Romancing notions
of heartfelt
decadence,
a prelude
to emotional
devastation...

If I should sing
a mournful lullaby
of shattered dreams
and all that is
forever lost…

Then know
I yearn
my passion's end
in an eclipse of
eternal darkness…

Forever
blown
on
Chill
Winds
of
Time
And
Memory…

Remember me…

# Set me free...

Horny as Hell,
but bound
by my abstinence
of an impossible
dream.

Passions stir
and fade,
rejecting
possibilities
in favour
of my illusions.
Fore they are
my comfort,
my sanctuary,
all that
I crave…

Life is for
the living
and I
no longer walk
among them,
fore I am a shadow
that was burned
by the light,
a ghost
that walks
in twilight
shades,
yearning
what could be
and not
what is.

Set me free…

# My Nuclear Winter...

Ashes swirl and dance
like snowflakes
from a
darkened sky
on a toxic
empty wind...
The signs were there,
alarm bells rang,
voices cried out,
fractured in the
imminent meltdown
behind my eyes…

Unseen
and unknown,
humanity fades
to ghosts
of memory
as perception
distorts reality
into fragmented
two dimensional
echoes,
desperately clinging
to cherished delusions,
wandering alone
in the harsh
nuclear winter of my mind…

# Soul Tragedy...

I'm so numb,
when did the lines
between
delusion
and reality
become so blurred?

The stars
are winking out,
The darkness
is coming,
I feel it
to my very core…

I'm so cold,
Abstinence
in my illusion
will not
let me
bow to temptation…

In my mind,
I see
the growing
atrophy
building
in the shadows…

I'm so broken,
wearing
a joker's mask
to feign
a semblance
of life to my peers…

Recoiling
from touch
yet yearning
for love
in a
contradiction of madness…

I'm so lonely,
Contact with
the living
fades
beyond
my reaching grasp…

Is there
anybody out there?

# Broken Toy...

Goosebumps…
Clamped teeth
Shiver…
Clenched fist
Razor tingles
over
quivering flesh…

Do it…
Quickly…
Now!!!
Arousing me…
Seducing me…
A moment of feeling
amidst numbed senses…

Voices…
taunting,
craving…
Perceptions blur,
a moment of weakness
distorted in
resolute thoughts…

Disjointed…
Anointed…
Prince of delusion,
See me squirm,
facing ever
changing realities
like a noose
about my neck…

Choking me,
Engulfing me,
Consuming me…
The glint
of my blade
has never
been so appealing…

Kiss the demon,
Pins and needles
bite hard…
Potential futures
explode in a storm
of visions dreamt
in narcoleptic lullabies…

Broken toy, damaged beyond repair…

# Walk Away...

Do not wake
my demon, boy…
Walk away…
NOW!!!
Whatever petty gripe
you hold, Let it go…
I do not
want your blood
on my hands…

If you truly
wish your last sight
to be me,
watching
the life fade
from your eyes,
then so be it,
continue on this path…

But let it not
be said
that I didn't give you
the choice…
He is stirring…
Last chance…
Walk away,
Lest I quell
your beating heart…

What is it to be?

Too late…

# Twix't Hope and Despair...

Always looking behind
to find the way forward…

Clarity fades in a fog of
relentless uncertainty,
clouding the path we walk,
masking the choices
we make…

All we are, defined
in dreams we strive
to achieve, fading in
greater insecurities,
lost to abundant woes…

Hope, our constant
companion,
caught twix't life
and despair,
struck comatose
of substance,
snuffed in soft whispers…

Decaying in a
fragile mind,
Awaiting
resurrection,
to be
awakened,
unforeseen
in the kiss of an Angel…

# Losing My Illusions...

Reality jars,
stopping me
in my tracks…
This illusion,
I've nurtured
for so long,
burns to ash
in the quietus
of my dream,
crumbling
in my hands,
slipping
through
my fingers
like dry sand,
blown away
to dust on an ill wind…

I stand
on the edge
of the void,
tasting of its
sulphured
intoxication,
no more
than a shadow
to its storm
to be
absorbed
by the darkness…

So long
have I held
my demons at bay,
futile
in my efforts…
Always,
they taunt me,
call to me,
beckon me…
Now I find myself
craving
their embrace,
a moth to the flame…

Wings burning
in the light
of truth,
falling through
an ashen sky,
grey in its
uncertainty,
devastated
in its rage,
numb
in its aftermath…

Living a lie
in servitude
of a
false God…

Losing my illusions…

# So Very Tired...

Holding on…
Coping…
Suppressing
emotional traumas
in a blanket
of denial
that panders
delusion…

So many voices…
When did their
aggregation
become
so abundant?
When did
they become
so strong?

Restless…
Sleepless…
Always
waking me,
exhausting me,
wearing me down…
Red rims frame
shadowed eyes…

I am such a mess
My demons
plot their
subjugation
of my corporeal
cognizance
I'm so very tired

Please let me sleep…

# Cold Tears...

Dim in the candle lit darkness,
squinting through blurry eyes,
repressing tears that well
in the light of truth…

Illusions fade in hostile isolation,
cut like the strings of a marionette,
mournfully numb in the loss
of serenity's dream…

Deceiving myself, lost to my purpose,
suppressing flesh bound desires,
recoiling from intimacy's touch
in fear of being burned…

Voices rage in a storm of clarity,
unwelcome in their awakening,
carving rictus smiles in my taut pelt,
spilling my blood…

Touching on a dark, empty void,
crooked in perception's falsehoods,
walking through a broken mind,
captive to my solitude…

# A Schizophrenic Plea...

If thou shouldst look
beyond thy
preconceived notions
of that which thou
doth behold in truth,
then behold me
for who I am
and not in the contempt
my kind doth rise in thee.

I am but a man
and though my mind
be touched by madness,
art thou really
so different from I?
I doth bleed, I doth cry,
I doth eat and I doth sleep.
Couldst thou see the man
beyond the madness?

Open thy mind,
embrace me
as thou wouldst
thy brother.
Fore I shalt
burden thee not,
I wouldst wish only
to be equal
to thine eyes.

Thy contempt be shadowed
only by thine ignorance,
for if thou wouldst judge me,
then I beseech thee,
judge me not
on thy preconceived notions,
but upon mine actions
and upon my words
as a man of equal standing.

But beware, judge not lest ye be judged thyself…

## <u>Psychic Psychosis……</u>

Spectres in the unseen darkness,
lacking substance, gaining strength.
Whispered voices, raging shouts,
questioning, telling and unyielding.
Sepulchral shadows cast in empty rooms,
forsaken by time and memory.
Awakened and drawn by insomniatic lullabies.

Prophetic dreams, eclectic visions,
altered states of consciousness and self.
Thoughts transcending space and time,
blurred, chaotic and confused.
Unwritten potentials of infinite choices,
confined in metaphysical reality.
Conceived, perceived, and sensed by few.

Unknown faces revealed,
in perception's twilight mood swings.
Projected thoughts from faceless crowds,
emotional bombardment in the wake of strangers.
Overcrowded in solitude, deafened in silence,
Death's sonnet written through living flesh.
Fated… gifted… cursed…

And shrink's diagnose it as schizophrenia...

# Losing the plot...

So blind to all
but my illusions,
perceptions
of physicality
fall by
the way side,
floating
like petals
on the winds
of change,
drawn deeper
into the abyss,
clawing
in the darkness
but grasping
naught
but my own
fractured
quintessence,
drowning
in my own
sagacity,
amaurotic
to totality

Succurro mihi…

# Hostile Isolation...

Such restless slumber
that stirs my clandestine thoughts,
there is more to perceive
beyond celestial divination
than the mind
that dares to dream.

I awaken, bathed in the light
of the rising dawn,
the stink of humanity
seeping from my pores,
like a disease that kills
the Earth that spawned it.

What cruel turn of fate is this?
That would see me born to such a savage child race?
That would bind me to such needs as I must deny?
That would make me crave
another's touch that is so far beyond my reach?

I am losing myself, unravelling in the tapestry of life,
threadbare to illusions of grandeur,
trodden underfoot to a juncture of malcontent.
How far must I fall? How much must I fade?
How long must I endure?

I am sequacious to the seeing eye,
yet foetal to the glare of shadowed eidolon,
lost in the depths of virulent solitude,
exiled to exist, perchance to live.

And truly, I want to live…

# Twixt Angels and Demons...

So disjointed,
anamnesis is always the first to yield.
The present dispersed amidst fading yesterdays
as tomorrow becomes today
and all I know is lost to dreams,
quelled before the inquisitor
of perception's vacillation.

I walk amidst fragmented thoughts,
a fractured man in a broken mind,
a stranger in my psyche,
building walls of self deception,
staving a path twixt Angels and Demons,
tainted in the purgatory of my soul,
torn between the darkness and the light
yet bound to intuition I cannot trust.

For what is reality?
If not but an assumption of the many,
bestowed by the few, conceived by the one
who sees beyond the veneer
of discerned corporeality?
Delving deeper beyond the veil,
lost to chimeras that hold revelations
and falsehoods in equal abundance.

A gift that keeps giving yet becomes its own curse....

...Caveo appositus obscurum...

# Barely Human...

I'm losing my humanity,
my élan vital has become so very inclement.
I can't seem to care
about anything anymore.
Things that meant the most to me,
that moved me and stirred me
from gelid depths, just sink me deeper,
pulling me under and I fight it no longer,
the war is over and I am culpable
to naught but my own compunction.

Brittle thoughts crumble to dust,
whispered away on an ill wind
that sighs like the icy breath
of waking Winter.
I stagger blindly, forever falling
through harsh brumal wastelands,
adrift amidst fickle contentions,
lost to abundant woes that lose their bite
in shards of splintered truth,
numb to all that once made me human.

Choking on fumes of despair,
noxious in their toxicity,
drowning in an ocean
of fetid despondency,
losing myself in a cataclysm
of my own making,
numb to a life of fragmented spectres,
congealing in neglect of all
that once made me whole.

And I really couldn't care less...

# Madness and Solitude...

Exiled by my own bequest,
a victim of my flaws,
abjuring further
and further away,
losing hope, losing self,
recoiling from touch
but craving love
in a conflict of need
and inability to connect,
a contradiction of desire
in self-induced isolation.

Locution cannot convey
the depth of my
phrenic malaise.
Slipping through the cracks
of acumen as lucidity
loses coherence,
decaying to instability
in it's lack
of consummate solidity,
mixing volatile cognition
with raw emotion
in a cocktail of
reasoned seppuku.

Days pass to weeks in a
symphony of silence,
lost to an abundant
overture of thoughts,
given an aria of voice
in an orchestra of despair,
deafened in a crescendo
of night whispers
that cantillate
a desolate berceuse
on the event horizon
of a collapsing essentia.

Did I ever feel any other way?

# <u>Adrift Amidst Changing Yesterdays...</u>

Memories fade,
shifting in the light
of changing
yesterdays,
losing
quintessence
in a fiction
of self belief
that builds illusion
in a plight
of honed denial.

No more
may I build
chimera certainties
atop kaleidoscope
dreams,
standing boldly
on clay feet,
set to dissipate
through
the hour glass
like sand slipping
through
my open fingers.

Plunging me
deeper
into an abyss
of self loathing
and loneliness
that strips me
of my gifts
and leaves me
empty
in a storm
of my own
affectation.

Rage courses
through
the void
in a
maelstrom
of malign
voices,
leaving
me numb
in the wake
of their
sublime touch.

Forever falling through the darkness,
lost to evanescent certitudes…

# An Epiphany in Celibate Onanism...

Pleasures of the flesh
distract from creations
of the soul...

My temperance
that has long
been my bane,
a burden of suppression,
denying my carnal needs
in wait of the one
who is worthy
of my attentions.

So long,
have I craved
her touch,
a fingertip caress,
a warm embrace,
a yearned for kiss,
a night of untold passion
to douse the flames
of desire.

My resolve weakens,
endeavoring
to solitary pursuits,
conducting
a solo symphony
in the art
of genital persuasion
to sate such
lascivious drives.

Yet still I am unhappy,
plagued by maudlin thoughts,
melancholy in my loneliness,
mournful to my inability
to connect with others
that slips
further and further
from my grasp.

I've got to be strong…

Yet from my frustrations,
virtuosity rages from within,
rising in a wave of sagacity
that burns a trail
through my mind,
exploding in a blaze
of softly penned words,
scribing dreams and voices
in a heart of passion and
boundless potentialities.

And so I realize
in an epiphany of
divine clarity
that we all suffer
for our art
and through endurance
and acquiescence,
we live beyond our days
in words etched from our pain,
beheld in the pages of eternity.

Ergo, I live forever…

# Aberration...

So long do I wait,
creating fictions
that are so much more
desirable than the world
that claims dominance
over my perceived reality,
embracing lives
in characterisations
that are so much more
appealing to my senses,
becoming a chameleon
to my dreams,
slipping further
and further away,
losing my sensations
of self in predilection
of all that I create
in anticipation
of who or what
I may yet become.

Changing realities,
changing perceptions,
changing the world
around me,
creating anomalies
in the streams
of causal nexus,
fighting the darkness,
embracing the madness,
loosing my demon
on a world of potentiality,
losing mastery over
the voices of eidolon,
scribing in the shadows
of sibyllic visions
of what I know should be
yet waking to worlds
that defy the verity
of fading yesterdays
in a paradox
of changing
tomorrows.

And so I weep,
mourning all
that is lost
in the eyes of fate,
holding destiny
in the palm
of my hand,
crushed
in the irony
that I was
not meant
to be

## Echoes in the Ghosts of Madness...

Cleansing my soul
in a baptism of fire,
burning in the darkness
that seeps through breaches
of fractured quintessence...

Folding to voices
that endlessly cry out
from the empty shadows,
such elusive eidolon
that call beyond the veil...

Manipulating my reality
in distortions of perception,
built on foundations
of falsehood, holding back the storm,
suppressing a fury that erodes the stones
of all I hold in axiom...

...Forever seeking cessation for my fading Élan vital...

# And So I Scream...

The Demon cries out,
banishing me
to the darkness,
his breath like frost
upon my heart,
his touch becomes
an eclipse
upon my soul…

So creative is he,
so artistic
in his games
as he begins
to ravish my mind,
leaving me deranged
and barely lucid…

The dreamscapes
he'll paint,
such lipstick lusts
lost in
groggy thoughts,
to fawn upon
my ethereal desires,
tainting them,
making them gritty,
livid in their fading…

…and so I scream…

# Drained...

...Drained...
...Lifeless... Numb...

Lost beyond the
dark perceptions
of physicality,
locked in a repetition
of troubled thoughts
that plague
and torment
in a storm
of obsessive turmoil...

Clawing from the depths,
raging to a fury unspent,
burned in a fire of truth
that shatters
illusion's comfort,
bursting the bubble
of hope
that held chimera dreams
so safe for so very long...

...Drained...
...Hollow... Empty...

Exposed beyond humility,
a shell that once held
such life and love
in such fervent ardor,
lays waste
in the purgatory
of paramnesia's waltz,
forsaken in the eyes
of vociferous solitude...

Like sand seeping
through a
fractured hour glass,
time loses its
linear chronology
as the dawning rays
of aurora's glare
gently warm
barren sightless eyes,
lost to the thrall
of phrenetic
night whispers...

...Tearless... Obtund...
...Drained...

# <u>Thin Ice...</u>

Do not presume
to know that what
I see is not real
because it is not
tangible to your eyes

Do not think
that what I hear
is a lie perceived
by my fears
in a chorus
of voices
in an orchestra
of madness

You skate on the ice
of causality,
never looking below,
embracing a
superficial surface
on a lake of perception,
oblivious to the depths
that stir beneath
your feet

I see your cold,
sterile world
above me
through the algid
crystal window,
frosted in a distortion
of two dimensional
reality, reflected
in the cracks
that form at the
edges of entropic physicality

The irony that you
believe me beneath  you
is not lost on me,
for though
I am born of the light,
I was cast to the darkness,
lost to the madness,
to speak its voice
through a looking glass
of fractured quintessence

And so I wait
as visions come to pass,
staving a path
twixt the shadows
of uncertainty,
beheld in the tears
of the Angels lament
in a fortress
of shattered dreams,
honed through
the sagacity
of a broken psyche,
beyond the empty lives
that skate above
the thin ice

And so, one by one…

…they will fall…

# Fighting my Nature...

My mind and body
in conflict,
one refusing
to acknowledge
what the other
so desperately needs,
a battle of wills
whose casualty is sanity...

The mind so sure
that love is unnecessary,
a temporary
hormonal imbalance
that drains finances
and distracts
from the greater
creative endeavors
that secure an illusion
of immortality...

The body, yearning,
primal in its needs,
unrelenting in its craving
to be touched, to feel,
to have, to hold,
beating the passion
of a poet's heart,
programmed
at the cellular level
before life began
as the mind
seeks to reboot
the system...

This war of body
and mind
that wearies the soul
in the battle waged
for dominancy
and supremacy
of will, restraint
and ideological victory
over human nature
versus
disciplined thought
in a temperance
of emotion…

But alas, it saddens me,
for there will be no victory
for either side,
tainting my soul
as my mind
stands to lose
its last vestiges
of passion
and humanity,
as my body loses
its ability to
connect with others,
a bitter irony
that either victory
will be hollow in its loss…

…I am so very tired of fighting my nature…
…Its breaking my heart…
…Its killing me…

…I have to end this…

# Evanescent Certainties...

I looked into the heart
of infinite darkness
and embraced
its sublime essence
as my own...

I gazed into the jaws
of eternity,
standing
on the threshold
of forever,
beheld in the glimmer
of the first thought
and watched
as the stars
burned
from the skies...

I have walked with Gods,
I have sung with Angels
and I have fought
with Demons,
dancing
with the Immortals
through Athanasia's
Twilight ballet...

But alas, all must
come to pass,
I have seen too much,
held too little,
I have lost so much
to the winds of time,
exhaled to dust
in a symphony of decay....

I was the Lord and Master
of Darkness,
I was the anointed Prince
of fictions,
I was the Keeper
of the Word
and I was the Bringer
of the storm...

I am a God,
bound in flesh,
a penance
of mortal frailty
that I may find humility
for my lack of compassion,
but this realisation
awakens such
pythonic anemnesis
that has lain dormant
for so very long...

Humanity is beneath me,
how can I feel clemency
when all about me,
they run rampant
like wayward children
in displays of cruelty,
greed and intolerance?
Betrayal is in their nature
and they will bring
their own destruction,
such disappointment
as they bring to me...

So much potential
evinced by so very few,
they poison me
with such
primitive emotions,
such affectivity
as I must purge
from my umbra
that it shames me
to wear their flesh,
the stink of humanity
seeping from my pores,
tainting my supreme
quintessence
in mockery
of my Godhood...

I can't live like this,
I'm fading away,
lost in the shadows
of my past,
my mind, too full,
as reality drifts
ever further
from my grasp,
memories replaced
by fictions
that are layered
and grafted
upon changing
perceptions,
building worlds
in the devastation
of time,
fulfilling a purpose
that strips me
of my acumen
til all I see
are abundant visions
so bold in their clarity
yet they distort faster
than I can scribe...

...Have I not suffered enough?

# Nevermore...

Behold me,
for I am broken,
my heart so cold,
lifeless where once beat
the passion
of a supernova soul,
an event horizon
that collapses
and guides me
on a destructive path
to temperance
in the ashes of love…

No longer
do I sing my adoration
in soothing lullabies
that drive
the demons
from my mind,
haunted by the hand of fate,
no longer do I feel
the yearning
of divine adulation,
nor crave the dreams
of what could be…

So lost, so alone
in the world once more,
dying in the light,
embracing the darkness
as the sands of time
slip through
my open fingers,
trod to dust
in the long cold embers
of the endless twilight Winter,
bitter in the discontented cries
of all that I have become…

…all that I have lost…

So numb, so empty,
the hollow man cries out to love…

"...Bequeath me nevermore..."

# ...The Demon is Awake...

The Demon is awake…
No more do I suppress him…
Oh no, his time has come
as he knew it would
and I embrace him
with open arms…

He intoxicates my mind,
burns his mark
upon my soul
in visions
of the chaos
he will bring
in my name…

He is the master manipulator,
the long game player,
the bringer of the storm
and you are exposed
before his eyes…

Such words of fatal truth
that push to press
the axiom bomb
that detonates
the maxim's toxicity,
exploding the shroud
of falsehoods,
beheld in the book
of stratagem…

For the pawns are rife
in the trinity of mind wars
and your games
of validation
become the
Demon's
playground…

You will see
how creative
this genius can be
as the Demon
tears your world apart,
brick by brick,
layer by layer
in subliminal ideas,
stray thoughts
and metaphoric rage
in divine retribution…

You won't even know
the game is afoot,
but you can stop this…
The truth will set you free…

But alas, this is not who I am
or who I would wish to be,
the Demon is back
in his box
so be thankful
I am not a vengeful God…

…But…

…Beware the path you walk…

# <u>The Oncoming Storm...</u>

Beware the oncoming storm,
static charging RAGE
as electric tendril fingers
caress the TURBULENT cerebrum,
a CRY that rolls like thunder
to the tears of a TROUBLED sky,
torrential in its outpouring
from a DARKLING cloud
burst from a TAUT
medulla oblongata
to a bereft
ocean of sorrows,
such PAIN
as lightning cracks,
a bellow of devastation,
PULSE beating
through temples,
drumming
beneath fingertips
as FIRE ignites
swiftly behind
RED rimmed eyes
that struggle
to hold back a FURY,
so long repressed
in the decaying psyche
of a BROKEN mind...

...Ground Zero for the coming VOLCANO day...

# She…

# Beyond the Glass of Axiom…

So full of self loathing,
she can barely look at herself.
So many choices made in haste,
self serving in nature
as to leave her regretful
of consequence and shameful
to the sway of cause and effect.

So long has the darkness grown
inside her, devouring her essence
with such sublime relish,
that she craved it's touch
with such passion,
as it fed upon her soul,
fading the light in her eyes.

Lost in an ocean of lies,
adrift amidst deceptions of self,
tainted to the evil of her sins.
She drowns in her sorrows,
submerging deeper and deeper
into an abyss of realisation
that strips her of illusion.

Desperately she reaches out,
clawing her way to a surface
that grows farther and farther away.
Her demon rises to fill her skin,
glimpsed in a speculum of truth,
eclipsing her extrinsic beauty
as the veil of self perception falls.

# Transcending the Brink
# of her Supernova Soul...

A candle flame flickers
in the breeze
of an open window,
casting shadows
that dance on the walls

So still, she sits,
a statue of illusion
a single tear,
the only semblance of life,
seeps from stony eye

So long has she held on,
nurtured, embraced,
lived for her dream
with a clarity
she held in stone

Now all at once,
she is poisoned
by its deception,
numbed to its touch,
doubtful of its certainty

Sightless eyes
delve deeper depths,
grasping remnants
of its sway,
holding naught but falsehoods

She stands stoic
on a chimera landscape
at the event horizon
of her breaking mind,
lost to fading Utopia

She walks through
her garden of hopes,
each bloom, carefully tended
and brought to fruition
by her own hand,
shrivelling in the quietus
of her yearning heart

Her castle of dreams,
laid stone by stone,
a fortress of repose,
built to withstand
a siege of maxim,
crumbles to ruin
before a black hole sun

Silently, she waits,
beheld in the thrall
of an axiom supernova,
raging in a troubled sky,
that brings her world
crashing down around her,
'til she too, fades to nihility

Heart cold, empty shell,
hollow nonentity,
the statue weeps its last,
lost to catatonia's kiss

Candle flickers
to wisp of smoke,
snuffed to the wick
on a tenacious breeze
that draws a darkness
that consumes all

# The Coming Storm...

She painfully
walked
the twelve steps,
carrying her cross
to bare…
She winced
as a sorrowed tear
stung her cheek,
an omen
of the
coming storm…

She was weary,
embittered,
her heart heavy
to the lies
and humility
that her life
had become…
Rage coursed
through her pain,
numbed
to submission
in the
realisation
that the
deception
had been her own…

Her illusion,
so tightly held
had crushed
in her embrace…
Her dreams
shattered
to shards
of reality,
stabbing her
painfully
and deeply
in their truth…

A sharp gasp
escaped her lips,
blood trickled
from her palm,
pricked
by the thorn
of the rose,
released
to an ocean
of woes,
bidding farewell
to a galleon
of dreams…

# Insomnia, Self Harm, Addiction & Suicidal Tendencies…

# Sleepless.

Tick- tock, tick- tock, The day doth fade.
Click lock, take stock, Thy soul decayed.
Twilight, my night, The dark descends.
Take flight, make right, The cold ascends.

Thump, thump, thump, thump,
mine heart doth speak.
Hard lump, cold stump,
My pain doth peak.
Like gas, no mass,
It creeps and shrouds.
To pass through glass,
And sightless clouds.

I fight the night,
as shadows bleed.
My night, my plight,
My demons feed.
My mind, unkind,
My voices rage.
My bind to find,
A wordless page.

They call, I scrawl,
My fingers bleed.
I fall, I crawl,
An end, I plead.
My brain in pain,
Bring forth the dawn.
insane, restrain,
Embrace the morn.

# Happiness is a Cold Razor.

The darkness building up inside,
My mind and flesh are numb.
So cold this shell, in which I dwell,
And so my demons come.
Why can't I feel no joy, no pain,
My God, I'm dead inside.
I need to end this living death,
My senses have denied.

A sharpened blade on naked flesh,
It rests before the slide.
I take a breath, defy the death,
And let the razor glide.
A line is formed in razor's wake,
As blood stampedes the slit.
It drips and runs, it stings and stuns,
A recess from the shit.

I feel again, I smile and cry,
I need to go again.
I place the blade back in the slit.
So deep, so strange, Amen!!!
The flesh is warm, the blade is cold,
And so my senses reel.
An alien tip inside my flesh,
There must be more to feel.

I lay back holding hand to wound,
Like a junkie with a fix.
I laugh and cry, I smile and wince,
My brain needs pain for kicks.

# Insomnia.

So tired, so wired,
Can't close my eyes and settle.
My mind defined,
My blood tastes sharp like metal.

I wander far inside my mind,
A door ajar, a path that winds.
Questions, questions, thoughts and deeds,
So weak, so meek, so full of needs.

My throat so dry, my eyes they hurt,
My head like lead, my mind alert.
Outside the corner of my eye,
The shadows move and dance and fly.

I hear the voices call my name,
So full of hate, so full of blame.
I need a fag, I need to sleep,
I need a drink, I need to weep.

# <u>Withdrawal... (Intense Rhyme)</u>

Medication gone,
my mind is growing stronger,
Dedication done,
my days are growing longer.
Destined hopes, so far away
and yet so close to feel,
Jesting gropes in fields of grey,
sustain me with their zeal.
Immortal thoughts and demon song
possess my waking mind,
A portal caught in semen strong
assess my quaking bind.

Darkened thoughts and shadows cold,
I touch upon the void,
Harkened naught and mad behold,
so much has been destroyed.
Agitate and feral needs,
suppress the beast within,
Vegetate and peril feeds,
oppress, bequeath, give in.
A reckoning not far away,
to cleanse and bleach the mind,
Beckoning a worthy prey,
so dense in breach decline.

Forsaken ghosts of shadows past
arise in slumbers void,
Awaken most in shadows cast,
despised in lumbers toyed.
A new day dawns upon my mind,
dispelling wisps of fear,
A clue that mourns my shadows bind,
expelling lisps and tears.
To face a foe of inner born,
eternal fates unkind,
To place a blow that sinners mourn,
external hates decline.

## Everthing's fine...

Shattered bones and teeth are broken,
Scattered lies and thoughts unspoken.
Onward raging clarity,
A timeless moment fractured slowly.
Drown me in this place I find,
Beyond my soul, beyond my mind.
Phase me into altered state,
Face to face with all my hate.
Hostile isolation brings,
Darkest thoughts with hidden strings.
Cut the flesh, suppress the pain,
Kill the voices in my brain.
Stirring echoes build inside,
Thoughts and wants and needs denied.
Friends and lovers lie and stray,
Cut me deep as they betray.

...But apart from that, everything's fine...

# Hollow Man...

Twisted knots of fear within,
this cramped and foetal frame.
Flesh is ripe for cutting now,
as demons call my name.
A single tear is all that comes,
there must be more to feel.
Why must it always come to this?
As blood and thoughts congeal.

Cigarettes with embers bright,
goose-pimpled blistered skin.
Fighting off delusion's grasp,
and surfaced thoughts within.
Illusions born in fantasy,
cascade inside my mind.
Why do I blind myself to truth?
And all delusions find.

Shattered dreams and splintered mind,
with thoughts all left unspoken.
Suppressed inside, alone, denied,
discarded toy so broken.
Emotions numb in blackest void,
fragmented shards of pain.
Despair, the rising demon songs,
that dance within my brain.

# Hollow Quest...

My quest to chase the Dragon,
Inhale of her sweet soothing aroma
Selling my soul...
Sweating... yearning... pain...
I weary of the hunger...

My lady leaves me craving her,
Can't eat... can't sleep... so wired...
My kingdom for a horse...
Shaking... fever... cramps...
Flea on a hot plate...

The quest goes badly,
The king is unimpressed...
Chills... goose-bumps... tears...
Pebble-dashing the porcelain throne...
Face in the mud or at least the chance...

My elusive nemesis, Skag...
My best friend, Harry...
Behold Excalibur divide the spoils...
The silver flute quickens my heart...
Hit me... fix me... toot me a tune...

The alchemist whose flame,
Turns dust to elixir,
White to brown...
Enthral... captivate... intoxicate...
Smack me down hard...

Today's episode was brought to you by the number '1'
and sponsored by the letter 'H'

# Farewell to Fading Quintessence...

…TOO MUCH…

…It's all just TOO much…

...My HEAD... Throbbing...

...Temples POUNDING

through fingertips…

…TOO many voices
filling my MIND,
unsavoury thoughts
tainting my SOUL
in an aura of darkness
that CREEPS throughout
my WHOLE being,
poisoning ME
to my CORE…

HOW did it come to THIS???

…Please HELP me…

…I've tried to be
a GOOD man…

…God only knows…

…I've TRIED…

Is this ALL there is???

Waking in a world
that's NOT my own,
LOST in a maelstrom
of shifting realities,
SHOUTING at shadows,
unveiling agents
of CHAOS
in the EYES
of innocence...


SINKING in an abyss
of despair,
dragged on a TIDE
of illusion,
building WALLS
to HIDE the PAIN
in proclamation
of my MADNESS…

…I can't do this anymore…

# The Beginning of the End...

So suddenly the storm breaks…
With such disdain, the voices rage
as crimson tears fall,
so pure against the stark scream
of a broken mind,
finding belonging
in a tide of shattered dreams,
choking on the ashes of promise,
an end that feels so near
but never comes…

Emphatic whispers in the silence
as hate bubbles below the surface,
obsessing trivialities
that call for revenge
on those that trespass against us,
hollow apologies that
appease the guilty hearts,
too little, too late,
crying in the solitude,
for empty words are never enough…

Chaos bleeds from the scars of emotion,
unseen to the eye,
oblivious to the dying soul,
cutting so deep inside,
evolved by compulsions
that become absolute,
a mistake to be made over and over
and so fingertips gently caress
the revolver's cold metal surface,
drawing it toward me…

Life is a privilege to those
with the courage to stay and live it,
but that is not me…
I am so alone,
each day I disguise my thoughts
behind a pompous smile
as my mind crumbles a little more,
blurring the boundary of reality,
breaking my will to fight
before an inquisition of pain…

The way out is obvious, even to me…
It is the beginning of the end,
such grave thoughts
in the midnight of my soul,
my body covered
in an abundance of fading scars
like a map that draws a path
that swiftly leads me here…
to this moment… this place… this hour…

pushing the barrel up under my chin,
I close my eyes
and……………………………

# Ya really wanna know?

I'm not here to debate
the intricacies
of right and wrong…
I'm not going to justify
the choices
of my actions…
I'm just going
to tell you why…

I cut to feel
when I'm numb
to my core,
just for some
semblance of living
that tells me
I'm still alive…

I cut to suppress
the demons
in my head,
when their
loathing of me
becomes too much
to bare…

When they tell me,
I don't deserve
to live, that death
is an option
I haven't got
the decency to take

The dead whisper
in my ears,
beckoning me,
calling me, telling me
what to write
They know who I am…
They know how I feel…
I don't want
to be gifted
I don't want
to be different

I'm sick to death
of reading minds,
projected by strangers…
I've had enough
of eclectic dreams,
potential futures
I can't change…

I'm tired of fighting
my mind,
of not being able
to connect with people…

I'm tired of wearing
a mask…
I'm tired of voices
in my head,
of living in illusions,
of living in fear
I'm tired
of being lonely
I hate who I am…

I don't want your pity
I don't want your help
I don't want to be your
good deed of the day…
I write these words
not for you, but for me
I write them for clarity
of thought and mind…

I write them for the day
when I stop being
a coward
and have the courage
of my convictions
to take that final leap
to find the peace
I crave…

Don't judge me, everyone lives to die…

# Fritz O'Skennick

# Hi, I'm Fritz O'Skennick...

You've asked me to explain my name,
So I'll attempt to try.
It's more than just a name to me,
And here's the reason why.
It speaks in cryptic, rhyming voice,
On sight for all to see.
If they should choose to see my soul,
And know what's plaguing me.

It speaks of darkest thoughts within,
Embodies what I do.
It gives me strength performing works,
Unknown by those who view.
It gives me life and sings my songs,
Awareness raised through art.
It helps me do what I must do
In life to play my part.

It shows I have a sense of fun,
I'm not afraid to smile.
To laugh at life's ironic twists,
And scribe my thoughts a while.
It tells of voices in my head,
You see, I'm schizophrenic.
And that is why my user name,
Is simply 'Fritz O'skennick'.

# Dear Psychiatric Nurse,

Please don't force me onto meds,
There must be other ways.
To calm the demons in my head,
And ease me through my days.
Let me prove beyond a doubt,
The works that I must do.
See me thrive, creating worlds,
And writing words anew.

The meds suppress my heart and soul,
A stranger in my head.
I couldn't bare the living death,
Of thoughts and words unread.
I'd rather die than lose my mind,
An empty, hollow shell.
Where once creation laughed and played,
And whispered verses dwell.

I'm not a cliché or a stat,
Although I'm schizophrenic.
Log in to AllPoetry,
And type in Fritz O'skennick.
Here you'll find my many works,
Behold my soul laid bare.
Words of fiction based in truth,
Of thoughts and dreams I share.

You'll find I'm really not so bad,
Despite my altered states.
To write emotions raw and true,
Dispel my passing hates.
Please, I beg you from my heart,
Take the time to see.
My music, stories, poetry,
And plays defining me.

Please, just look…

## <u>Fritz O'Skennick (Acrostic)</u>

Friendly in my thoughts and deeds
Relaxed when on my own
Intellect to feed my needs
To scribe the thoughts I've sown
Zealous when my demon stands
On words and truth unkind
Sing my songs as he commands
Know now, he's in my mind
Embracing darkness from within
Now comes the time to write
No more a slave to thoughts therein
I'm free to feel the night
Can't sleep for ghosts that call wherein
Keep writing til its light…

# Acumen of a Dark Writer...

I scribe from voices in my head,
that speak the Demon's rage.
All my darkest thoughts are bled,
in words upon my page.

Blinding me with visions dark
until the words are penned.
Softly spoken words so stark
and darkness without end.

Glimpsing worlds beyond my mind,
that hurt and take their toll.
Am I the Demon here defined
who's feeding on my soul?

I hear the voices of the dead,
who come to me to speak.
To tell their tales in words unsaid,
my damaged mind unique.

Whispers in the twilight time
and even through the day.
Words so clear and so sublime,
while others cause dismay.

Overwhelmed, they haunt my mind,
they have no one to hear.
Thoughts and deeds become entwined
in words so soft and clear.

I write to quell the Demon's hold,
to keep the dead at bay.
I watch as darkest words unfold
in beauty and decay.

I'm not writing to deceive,
but ease the many voices.
Its up to you if you believe,
the world is full of choices.

My shrink said I am not to blame,
you see I'm schizophrenic.
And this why I chose my name,
My name is Fritz O'Skennick...

# Facets...

The master poet,
so full of passion,
strength and desire,
bearing his soul
to the world
in profound rhapsodies
bestowed by his love
of the written word…

The damaged musician,
riddled with insecurity,
expressing his heart
in a plethora
of melodies
that haunt,
taunt and rage
in a distortion
of whimsical clarity…

The prolific writer,
creating worlds
and giving life
to the souls
who'll live there,
a God who decrees
every action
but allows his creations
enough free will
to guide the plots
that bind them
to his imagination…

The eccentric actor,
a chameleon
bringing life
to the words
of the writer,
striving for credibility
in the masks
that he'll wear
to the watchers
of his beloved craft…

The egotistical performer,
a visible sentience
to the poet
and the musician,
expressing their art
with a passion
that reflects the soul
of the actor yet differs
in translations
of changing continuity…

The lonely schizophrenic,
bounced around
the mental health system,
desperately trying
to be whole
amidst an army of voices
and delusional states
that plague his fragile,
fragmented mind,
but he fights his demons
to hold a truce of reason
to live another day…

The wary psychic,
sensitive to the ripples
and cracks in reality,
lost to visions
that are as prophetic
as they are misleading
as the eidolon
breach the bough
of the quiet time,
each so desperately
wanting to be heard
on a path between
the darkness and the light…

The doting father,
the dutiful son,
the sibling rivalry,
the best friend,
each rejecting
the role
of the
fading lover,
sacrificed
that the others
may thrive without
the complexities
of distraction
and hormonal cravings
that burden the mind,
crush the soul
and break the heart…

A fractured persona,
living so many lives,
wearing so many masks
that conflict
in the choices made,
defining the boundaries
in the facets
of all that he perceives,
all that he was,
all that he is
and one day
all that he will become…

And so he seeks salvation
in the alignment
that will
make him
whole,
holding
the
hope
that
one
day…

…he'll be a real boy…

# The Virtuoso Dilettante…

Behold the hellacious rhapsodist…
Genius or mad-man?
So little contact with a world
of contradictions and lies,
he makes his own truth,
creating his own worlds
that defy the boundaries
beyond the inconsistencies
that lie in actuality.

His fictions so real as to fight
perceptions in his physicality,
screaming for an existence,
beyond the unspoken thought,
beyond the written word,
beyond peripheral shadows
that dance and play
in the twilight hours,
beyond the calling voices
that bid him to scribe their tales,
beyond the visions
that haunt his waking mind.

He withdraws ever further
from a world of betrayal
and uncertainty,
delving deeper and deeper within,
no longer bound to constrictions
of reality's falsehoods,
no longer tied to perceived existence,
he embraces his nature,
realising that truth
is but a perception
created by others
in a conviction of blind illusion.

He sits alone
in the flickering candle lit darkness,
unafraid, he ponders, he smiles,
he summons his demons,
lost to his visions,
he calls to the voices…

He presses quill to parchment…

And writes…

# Meet Me in Dreams of Forever...

...Behold my words for they are my heart...
...Behold my poetry for it speaks my soul...

And so I shall live
far beyond my time,
far beyond the
superficial fads
that die a meaningless death
in endless repetition
of relentless themes,
regurgitated
to the flock's juvenal
and engaged by
the age's mutton
robed as lamb...

I am a creator...
I am a writer...
I am a poet,
behold my words
for they define me
in their truth...

Cherish them,
for within their voice
you will find me
and share of me,
that we may hold
union as minds touch
in transcendence of time...

For as you read from my thoughts
and memes, scribed in
fading yesterdays,
so my words will be fresh
to your dreams of today,
embracing new tomorrows,
slowly bridging the expanse
of forever,
turning the pages of eternity,
that bring me life once more...

You bestow me
immortality,
for as you read me,
you will find me,
hold me,
and touch
upon my soul...

Remember me
and I shall live
on in you,
a notion, an idea,
an inspiration,
a legacy of perpetuity
as I commune
my thoughts
from ages passed
to you this day...

My legacy to you of my tomorrows
is your gift to me today and for this...

...I humbly thank you...

# ...Fuuuuuuuuuck You!!!

Do not censor me,
do not restrict me,
do not tie my hands
to conform to the ideals
of feckless fucking fools...
Do not expect me
to sit back and kiss arse
to appease your ignorance,
nor scribe my words
in hollow dreams
that are not my own,
to embrace
the idiot masses...

I would rather slap jam on my cock
and bang it into a bee hive
or gently rest my testicles
in a sleeping lion's mouth
and wedge my thumb up his arse
before I sell out to needy, greedy,
selfish, money grabbing bastards
and corporate yes men,
out to ride my coat tails
to pave a path
to fortune and success,
corrupting my talents
to make their money
in distortions of my dreams
as some sniveling, snot nosed,
cock sucking leech
without a soul
takes credit for my gifts...

My words are my own
and will always be true
to who I am,
without compromise
or compassion
for PC bullshit
or bubble wrapped niceties,
thrust upon us
for no other reason
than to enforce
repetitive conformity
and quell creativity
in hopes of trapping us
in the box,
without the will to think
outside of the fucking thing...

They can try
and they will fail,
for none
can stifle the thoughts
that lie within,
nor compromise my integrity,
nor distort my perceptions,
nor steer my fictions
to packaged popularity
or repetitive formulas,
nor corrupt my heart
in temptations
of riches or status or power...

I am who I am, take me or leave me,
I write what I write, read it or don't,
Let history be my judge,
let time breathe my words,
let the future bring me to life,
let eternity be my legacy...

...And if that is not good enough...
## ...WELL FUUUUUUUUCK YOU!!!

## <u>Waiting...</u>

Always stood
at the crossroads of life,
choices to be made,
left or right?
Darkness? Light?
Or maybe the grey
that flows between...

Sell my soul
or just have it crushed?
So many choices,
so little time,
so much to do…

Yet still I stand,
unsure
of the path
I walk,
waiting for a sign
to lead me onward,
waiting for my life
to begin…

Did I miss it?

Would be just my luck… BUGGER!!!

# The Gospel according to Fritz O'Skennick (1:1-6)

i. And lo the Lord didst speaketh unto man "I bringeth life unto thee, I giveth love unto thee, that thou may findeth light in the path that thou wouldst walk, that thou may findeth truth beyond the lies of man"

ii. "Beware the pride of man's folly, for he shalt corrupt the word of God, he shalt befall great evils unto the world in blasphemy of the lord's name, he shalt kill in the thousands and claim it be his will"

iii. "The words of the apostles siphoned by the ages, reformed, rewritten, reinvented that wouldst hold sway to beliefs that embrace bigotry and hate and war. Fractured in twain to fragments of interpretation and perceptions of false belief, spawning new faith of the one God that walk the same path yet diverge in the hearts of the faithful, a divide of intolerance."

iv. "And so in the shadows of change, the message fades to a book of contradictions. Distortions of peace bestowed in faith become weapons of corruption and judgmental stone casting as the self-righteous take arms in the name of power and hypocrisy"

v. "For though thy faith holds strong, quote not in judgment nor in temptation but in faith, that all may know the word of God and find love on the path of virtue. Embrace your fellow man as your brother, judge not of his sin but love of his soul and pray he sees wisdom in your words"

vi. "The message is as it has always been, love, honor and respect. Listen not to zealots and infidels who preach hate, war and death, for they do not speak in God's name, they know not what they do. In pride, greed and lust, they will fall and in tribulation, they will be judged"

# This is who I am...

I suffer from schizophrenia…
Now I realize a lot of people's reaction to that will be 'knife-wielding maniac', 'Norman Bates', 'Hannibal Lecter' or even 'Texas Chainsaw Massacre'.
Trust me when I tell you 'I've heard them all before'.

Now, don't get me wrong, I don't blame you in the slightest for feeling that way, for this is how the media portrays us. But the reality is that that stereotype only applies to a small percentage of us. To believe otherwise invites the same mentality and prejudice that preaches that all Muslims are terrorists or all Catholic priests are paedophiles. All autistics are like 'Rainman', or all gay men wear leather caps and have big handlebar moustaches.

It is simply not the case. We are all different. I believe that people with mental illness are an unrecognized minority group who cannot fend for themselves. As a result of this, they are victimized by a system that refuses to understand or even tolerate them.

In Britain, they are trying to pass a 'Bill' that states 'anyone registered as having any form of mental illness can be detained without ever having done anything wrong, institutionalized and force-fed anti-psychosis drugs.'

In essence, stop the crime before it happens and strip a quarter of the population of their civil liberties and basic human rights. The very thought of this terrifies me. I have never so much as been in trouble with the police and I don't have a violent bone in my body.

Yet if they pass this 'Mental Health Bill', I could be taken off the street or from my home, detained and institutionalized without trial, provocation or even defense. The fact that it gains more support each time it rears its ugly head is testament to the ignorance of the masses…

…Terribly sorry, I've strayed off the path (cancel rant mode). Yes, I have schizophrenia. Yes, I have voices in my head. And yes, I can be prone to delusional states and disturbing thoughts. But this is why I write, this is why my fictions become so intense as to border on reality. Quite simply, however briefly, I live them…

I stopped taking my medication nine years ago, because writing in all forms has replaced it. I can't not write, I don't get writer's block because my mind is constantly active and will not switch off. Voices and visions have long plagued my sleep patterns and waking hours, fighting for dominance in my eyes and works. I take Zopiclone and cannabis to help me sleep, for a few hours peace, co-codamal to tame the headaches. I'm exhausted, but I'm never short of something to write.

Compared to most schizophrenics I am fortunate, because not all the voices in my head are malevolent. They whisper ideas and sometimes even entire passages in my ear as I write. They harmonize with me as I sing my songs; they even help me write my lyrics.

Yes, I have bad patches, but who doesn't? Yes, I have dark thoughts. Again, who doesn't? My strongest malevolent voices, I recognize as my 'Paranoia', 'Self-loathing' and 'Self-doubt'. They are my darkness to bare and in no way affect anyone around me.

When they'd strike I used to cut myself because it numbed their influence. Now I have more control over them, I read to distract me from the grip they have over me. That said, I wouldn't change them for anything. They are part of me and I would not be whole without them and not nearly as creative either. This is who I am, it can't be helped, changed or ignored.

The problem is other (so called normal) people. Friends who I believed would be around for life that have turned their backs on me when they've discovered what I am. Others have just taken advantage of me, stolen from me and shunned me. Simply because I am a nutter, I am not like them. I don't share their yob mentality, so I must be mad!

I have long held my own counsel and am very guarded as to who I reveal this too. I find it very hard to trust in the intentions and motives of others. But every now and then someone comes along that I recognize as a kindred soul or that I can't help but trust. And I am revealed before them, as I am revealed before you now.

You see? Now that I have opened up to you and stand before you unveiled…

…I am at your mercy…

Will you still be my friend?

www.ingramcontent.com/pod-product-compliance
Lightning Source LLC
Chambersburg PA
CBHW051835040426

42447CB00006B/535